CHESAPEAKE BAY
GOOSE MUSIC

To Rachel & Tommy

As you watch
the geese think of
this story

Roger Ethier   Love
Christmas   Santa
1995

Roger Ethier

Dedicated to
"Petite Mom"

Printed in the
United States of America
First Printing 1995
ISBN 0-9644924-3-1

Library of Congress Catalog Number 95-090261
Copyright 1995 by Folklore Press
Box 166
Mt. Vernon, Virginia 22121

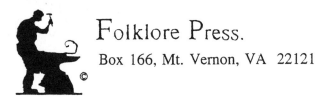

Folklore Press.
Box 166, Mt. Vernon, VA 22121

"They are embarked on a predetermined journey, these black migrants of the night, and come and go as though they carried chart and compass."

Introduction

A flock of Canada geese crossed the sky late last night, the first flight of the season. They were high up, over a mile and they sounded like a far away ship lost in fog, before the sounds faded in the south. After midnight, another flock came over, much lower...*"honk, honk, honk"*...they blasted the quiet night with their strong call, and seemed to be communicating with the civilization below and laughing at her at the same time. ...honk, honk, honk. By the time that these black migrants were out of earshot my decision was made. I was going back home to where the Canada geese are, to the place that I came from.

When you're raised on a farm you need to go back at least twice, perhaps three times a year. The relationships there, the quietness and smell of the land, the memories of the old folks, the persevering, faithful Canada geese and the other animals, all blend together to open up one's soul. Homes around cities are well manicured and the children are all combed and scrubbed but it's sort of sterilization coupled with constant never ending pressures from the city. It's a loop that never closes. It begins with a hollow feeling somewhere deep inside and then the loop starts spinning and mixes everything together, values, relationships, priorities. Suddenly everything is out of control. It's then that you need "a sorting out."

Chapter 1

With the sounds of the first Canada geese of the season, my youngest, Jeanne and I pack the cab of the pick-up well before dawn and together we head east, across the Virginia Tidewater to the Chesapeake Bay. It's late autumn and a blanket of frost covers everything.

Immediately the child slides across the seat and cuddles against me to keep warm. As we leave the city buildings are replaced by shoreline and fields and my mind races back thirty years to my life on the farm. In what seems to me only seconds a hundred snapshots reel through my head as vivid as if they were taken yesterday. In fact, what seems to me like seconds consumes nearly two hours and suddenly the dark outline of a large farmhouse appears just in front of us and stops, as I cut the engine.

Jeanne is excited and she quickly scrambles out of the truck and into the house, leaving me to carry our two overnight packs. By the time that I am inside, however Jeanne has escaped out the back door and into the barnyard where her grandmother has already begun her daily chores.

I follow her trail outside and as I look around in the early morning shadows for them, I reach down and scoop up a fistful of freshly plowed soil. When I stand erect again I'm already beginning to relax as I look out past the wooden gate into the field and spy my daughter and my mother.

An elderly woman talking with her grandchild looks across a field covered with five hundred Canada geese, her small flock of domestic hens intermingled with a few barnyard bantams, and her three shetland ponies, all feeding contentedly.

The farm people here are the salt of the earth," she says. "The land, the soil, and the fowl and animals are all in their blood."

The child looks up at her. She is not quite five feet tall, wears a red scarf around her head, and is bundled in a heavy cloth coat, thick woolen pants and socks, and leather shoes. Her face has few wrinkles, and her grey eyes smile when she talks.

Jeanne follows her in her chores. With her glove covered hand she reaches up and turns the rusty doorknob of the feed barn, a converted boxcar that years before her husband had hauled here and blocked into place high off the ground. The child watches as her grandmother walks across the floor to the grain bins with short firm steps and a slightly stooped back. Dipping into one of the bins, she scoops out a large pail of cracked corn and oats and the child hurries to follow as she carries the heavy pail outside to continue her chores. Walking through the field together, she explains the habits of the Canada geese.

"When ready to leave, the ganders, the males, early in the morning begin to toss their heads and flap their wings. One lone Canada goose then begins to honk, and then another and another until the excitement spreads throughout the flock. Almost simultaneously the flock then lifts off with great excitement and noise. They make one wide circle around the field and slowly form into a wedge and disappear, with the females leading the inverted "V" and the males protecting each of the two ends. "The honking in the distance reminds me of a freight train," she tells the attentive, listening child. "Here, on the bay we call the honking *Chesapeake Bay Goose Music*."

"At first, I didn't know much about Canada geese," she continues, "and so I went to the library to read everything that I could find about them. I learned that Canada geese mate for life.

Also, I found out that they are closely attached to their breeding grounds and seldom breed outside of their own group, choosing to return to the same place each year with the same mate. This flock has now returned here for the last thirty five years."

Jeanne is inquisitive, bubbling over with a thousand questions. "Ready to burst at the seams," as her grandfather used to say. Where do the geese come from? Where do they go? When did the first goose come here? And why do the geese keep coming back to this field, here on this farm every year? And there are many other questions. But she remains silent — but only for the moment.

Throughout the years her Grandmother has fed the flock and they have grown to accept her presence. Now the flock hardly shuffles as together, grandmother and granddaughter scatter cracked corn and oats on the ground among them. Both marvel at them as the elderly woman points out the long black necks, black heads and tails, and the large patches of pure white on their bodies.

"Notice," she says, "that many of them have white feet with mostly pure white bodies, with black wings and heads. They are very special, for they have the 'Marques des Rois,' the King's and Queen's markings, which are very elegant and also are very rare," she explains. "With the exception of the Canada geese that visit this field, this beautiful species is nearly extinct now. However, we are lucky, there are at least two goslings with the King's and Queen's markings born here each year."

As they continue walking through the flock, Grandmother points to a large goose. "By my estimates the wingspan of the elders tip to tip is seventy to seventy-five inches, greater than the height of most men," she says. "They weigh about twenty-five pounds each...and their honking sounds like a pack of baying hounds."

Later in the morning I'm waiting at the gate for my daughter and my mother to return. Their farm chores for the morning are nearly finished now and I watch as they walk back through the field hand in hand, followed by three ponies. On the way they stop and enter the hay barn which is filled with fresh hay that was harvested only a few weeks before.

Inside the fresh smell is as thick as a penetrating mist. Each grabs a large armful of hay before they step down out of the barn and scatter it on the ground for the ponies. Hesitating for a moment to run their fingers through the matted manes of the ponies and to talk to them, they then continue to the gate with her Grandma leading and talking all the while and the child listening and hurrying to keep up.

I open the gate and they pass through. Grandma is saying to Jeanne, "Canada geese are not native to this area. The

Great Atlantic Flyway is over sixty miles to the West, and it is very unusual for them to be here." She stops for a moment and the child catches up.

Finally, unable to hold back any longer, Jeanne blurts out in nearly a shout, "But Petite Mom..... the Canada geese, where did they come from, how did they get here, why do they keep coming back?" She slurs "Petite Mom" with a French accent so that it sounds like one word 'Tsee mom.' It's a name that has been used for two generations before her.

Her Grandmother looks intensely down at the child, smiles, and hesitates for a moment before speaking. "It's a story, Jeanne, that is very old and quite long. Perhaps your father will tell you," she says as she continues on to the farmhouse, leaving the child expectantly staring up at me.

"Petite Mom says that you know the story of when the first goose came here, Dad. She says that it happened when you were young, like me."

"Yes, I heard, Jeanne," I say as I take her hand and lead her to the rail fence. "Let's sit here on the fence and I'll tell you the story." I lift her up on a weather-worn wood rail and climb up beside her as together we stare out over the field of Canada geese and listen to loud, sweet *Goose Music*. And for the

next hour I tell her
the story of the
migration of
the first
Canada
goose to our
farm, and of
the three chil-
dren who
found him in
a snowstorm,
and of Petite
Mom who
cared for him.

Chapter 2

Far north, just below the icy Arctic region, there lies the great Island of Greenland. And on the harsh southwest coast of Greenland lies the Great Fjord. It is a large body of water, carved into great rock cliffs and extending inland nearly a mile, deep into the heart of the land. The water is sixty fathoms deep here and the weather is always by chance. Violent storms sweeping down from the Arctic in the winter and occasionally in the summer, cause the turbulent waves and deep swells to crash hard against the black stone cliffs in a perpetual assault.

At the breach, water sweeps into the inlet with a continuous thunder that rolls with the tide, and ends with a crack like a whip as the wave crashes against the face of the interior ledge. A quietness follows as the tide recedes, and the water flows back out into the bay to muster its strength for yet another charge.

No one hears the assault of the water, however, for this place is utterly desolate. In fact, it is one of the most desolate places on earth and no human being or mammal can survive here. Only in the three short months of summer is the rhythmic roar of the sea pierced by other sounds, for this is also the breeding and nesting grounds of migrant Canada geese.

Before the Eskimos, the Whalers and the Danish Explorers paused briefly and then passed this place by, the Canada geese were already here, having navigated from the south long before Greenland had fractured away from the continent.

Flying nearly a mile high, day and night, they followed the spring
thaw north, along the eastern coastline, pausing only
long enough each day for a short rest and to feed
in the marshes. Finally, after reaching the
Davis Strait, they crossed three hundred miles
of open water and came upon the Great Fjord
and the end of their two thousand mile trek.

   High on top of the most interior
ledge of the fjord, they land on a large, fertile
plateau spotted with fresh water ponds and
covered with thick, brown tundra. Already, the
migrants from the Arctic north, the Ptarmigan and
the Snowy Owl are here, and green shoots of grass and flowers are
poking through the tundra blanket, when the Canada geese finally

settle beside the largest of the ponds.

In a normal summer, the long days are ample for the routine drama of life and life's renewal to be played out, before the Canada geese abandon this place to the Arctic ice. But in the summer of 1951, large numbers of aircraft are flying over the Arctic to a war a half a world away. The entire earth seems in a tumult. The great air streams that control the weather suddenly change their course, and all summer long overcast skies and violent rain and hail storms pelt Greenland and the entire eastern coast of North America. Even the European continent is not spared from the violent, twisting winds. It is as if some great, heavenly force is flailing away in a demented rage over the bloody war that is blowing apart the bodies and lives of a half a million American, Korean, Australian and Chinese boys.

During the first four weeks of this violent summer, the geese deepen their nests and thicken the soft downy linings. On the outside of the nest, they construct thick walls of dried tundra grass for additional protection against the unexpected harsh elements. After the fourth week the goslings are hatched. However, they refuse to venture into the high winds and the ice covered tundra for their feed, choosing instead to remain near the nest.

But the feed near the nest is scarce by now, so, day after day and week after week the elders lead the goslings away to fresh feeding grounds nearby, with the hen leading the way and the gander following behind the brood.

The plateau is vast, yet outside of their nesting area all of the goslings mingle together to feed in a very tight pack, with the elders remaining on the outside. The youngsters look alike at first, but as they grow and develop feathers, their bodies are marked with distinctive patterns and colors which separate individual broods. Some inherit large black patches and others have deeper and richer colors. But one brood has exceptional markings this year, for both the gander and two goslings have pure white feet, with deep black wings and head. Along the coast at the feeding grounds, the watermen call these colors the King's and Queen's markings, for they are very elegant, indeed.

There are well over one hundred separate broods that have been hatched this year, over five hundred goslings. Yet, less than one hundred will ever leave this place. Of the three with the King's and Queen's markings, only one of the male goslings will survive, and he will never reach the southern feeding grounds.

The winds are too high and the ice which forms on their wings too heavy for the young birds. However, they must learn to fly or perish for soon they must start a two thousand mile trek south, to escape the impending freeze.

And so, as soon as feathers are grown, each gosling tries to fly despite the harsh weather elements. Some are blown out to sea, others are simply bashed against the stone cliffs of the island coast, too weak to cope with the winds. But others succeed and return to the nest to try a longer route the next day. And somehow, many survive and grow stronger and finally are ready for the migration.

The Arctic freeze has already begun when the Canada geese lift off and fly over the Great Fjord for the last time. As they fly out over the Davis Straits, they form an inverted black "V" against a heavily overcast sky. The largest geese lead the flock, their great, black heads thrust straight ahead, and the goslings follow behind, partially buoyed by the updrafts from the tips of the wings of the leaders. At first they fly low, below the threatening thunderheads, but as they continue over open water the weather clears and the lead geese climb to ten thousand feet, nearly the two-mile level.

Their migration will take nearly three weeks this year and buffeting cross winds will attempt to carry them inland, but their course will hold true as it always has. From the open waters of the Davis Straits they will reach the rugged Baffin Island coastline, choosing to remain over open water except to rest and to feed. Their heading will then change to southeast, along the Labrador coast, and then to south southwest across the Gulf of St. Lawrence, Nova Scotia and the Bay of Fundy to the northern coast of the eastern United States. Only half of the geese that departed Greenland will ever reach their destination in Cape Hatteras, off the North Carolina coast, however, for the rest will perish along the way.

Chapter 3

On a day when the Canada geese are winging their way south along the coast of Virginia, heavy snow is falling on a small farming community on the Chesapeake Bay. There, three excited children are making their way home from school. It's the first snow of the season, and school has let out early for the safety of the children. The oldest, a boy of eleven, turns around and shouts to his younger brother and sister who are trailing behind him. "Hurry up, it's getting colder and the snow is getting deeper!"

When he first turns, he expects to see his brother holding onto his younger sister's hand and the two happily chatting with each other as they always do while meandering on their way. But to his annoyance both have stopped and are walking off the road into the five inch deep snow. The oldest, Gene, immediately runs back to them and prepares to scold them and to hurry them along.

The girl, the youngest of the three, a first grader, is making her way through the snow, away from the road with her brother close behind. Her name is Carole, and her brother who is with her is named Jon. Both are heading for a small scrub pine tree and the mound of snow beside it. Carole stops at the mound and stares down as Jon comes up beside her. Both hesitate for a moment, then together they reach down and carefully scoop up the mound, snow and all.

When Gene
reaches them, the girl
is holding the bundle
of snow in her arms
and her brother Jon is
carefully brushing
the top and sides of
the snowy mass with
his mittened hand.
The girl turns back to
face her oldest broth-
er, and Gene stops
dead in his tracks.

The first thing that he sees is that his sister is holding a half-grown goose in her arms. It is white with large patches of black on its wings and has a large black head. At first he thinks that it is dead because its feathers are splattered with blood. His younger brother is brushing the snow away and attempting to find out where it is wounded and what is causing the steady stream of red fluid to drop on the fresh white snow.

The older boy's eyes move from the motionless bird to the faces of his brother and his sister. Both are covered from head to toe with snow that they have scooped up while picking up the bird, and the snow on them is speckled with red. Two sets of dark eyes, characteristic of their French Canadian heritage stare through the snow that covers their faces, to the half dead goose in the little girl's arms.

Gently he takes the goose from his sister and holds it in his right arm while with his left he probes under the wing for a wound. Then he stoops down and picks up a large handful of snow and presses it under the wing, holding it tightly, hoping that the bleeding will stop. The three of them are talking as he wraps the bird in his scarf, while at the same time he continues to press the wing tightly against the bird's body.

"What happened to him? Why is he bleeding so?" the young girl cries.

"It looks like he has been shot, and somehow we have got to stop the bleeding. Maybe the cold snow will help," Gene answers.

"I have never seen such a beautiful bird... look, his feet are white!" Jon exclaims as he continues to brush off the snow.

"Let's take the bird home. Petite Mom will know what to do," the little girl cries.

The girl is animated, full of life, and when she speaks she raises her outstretched arms, palms up, to the level of her shoulders and stares at her brothers, waiting for their approval. Her accent is French Canadian and she slurs Petite Mom so that it sounds like one word 'Tsee Mom.'

"Mais oui" the older boy says, and together the three of them tromp back through the snow to the road and then hurry to their home, with the older boy carrying the cloth covered bird and alternately running and walking, and the two younger children hurrying, hand in hand, close behind.

Chapter 4

The children run into the kitchen of the old farmhouse nearly exhausted, and stand there facing their mother, with the older boy holding the goose and the other two children standing on each side of him, lightly stroking the bird. Tears are running down the little girl's face, flowing into the crust of snow and mud that cover her reddened cheeks.

Across the large kitchen, a small woman looks up from two jars of canned tomatoes that she has begun to open. She has been sitting at a wooden table and rises when she first sees her children. She is short, just over five feet, her skin is smooth and light, and her eyes are grey and smiling. She is young and like her daughter is full of life. Her light auburn hair flows lightly over her shoulders as with short, firm steps she walks across the kitchen to her children and the wounded goose.

"Petite Mom, we found him in the snow," Carole says. "He's been hurt, and he hasn't moved since we found him."

"Well, let's take a look." And carefully she takes the goose from the arms of Gene. Pushing back the down and the feathers with her fingers, she quietly inspects the wounds on the breast and the wing.

"He is very weak and both his breast and his wing have been injured, but the bleeding has stopped," she says.

"Will he be all right, Petite Mom?" the girl asks.

"He has lost some blood, but it doesn't look like there are any other injuries.

The wound in his breast is not deep. We'll make a wooden splint and tape it to his wing to prevent any further damage. Here, boys, you hold the goose and spread the wing, and your sister and I will tape on the splint."

"What happened to him?" Gene asks, as his mother firmly tapes the splint into place.

"He's a Canada goose," she replies. "The bird was shot during its migration south. As you see, the bird is only half grown and most likely it grew weary while attempting to keep up with the rest of the flock. Gradually, it dropped farther and farther behind until finally it lost sight of the flock and its sense of direction. After it strayed off course, it most likely was spotted by a hunter while stalking pheasant in this area. After it was shot, it glided as far as it could, out of the range of the hunter, and landed exhausted and frightened where you found him."

"What shall we do with him?" Jon asks.

Looking down at the half grown goose, who during the last six months has survived the harsh Arctic ice and winds, and then traveled over a thousand miles through buffeting winds and  rain only to be shot after being separated from its flock, she hesitates for a moment, thinking of the flock which by now are approaching safe feeding grounds in the marshes of the Carolinas, and then says, "We'll put him in a large box here by the stove for the night, and tomorrow I'll put him in the barn with the hens where he will be warm and safe for the winter. But you all must understand he will never fly again because his wing is so badly shattered."

Petite Mom and the children fold a soft towel and place it in the box and then put the limp goose on the towel. By the time the children finish their homework and chores, the goose still has not moved. Each secretly says a prayer that the goose will get well, before they go upstairs to bed.

The little girl Carole, however, hesitates midway on the stairway, and then quickly runs back down and reaches into the box and softly pats the smooth feathers of the half grown goose.

"Dieu Tout Purissant apporte lui ta protection," she blurts out in a voice loud enough so that both the goose and God could hear her, before she runs back upstairs and into her bedroom.

In the morning, Petite Mom places the Canada goose in the barn where she also winters a small flock of laying hens, half a dozen bantams, four Mallard ducks, and a pair of domestic grey geese. During the first day, the half grown goose hardly moves and merely squats on the floor with its eyes closed.

"He'll pick up in a day or two and start eating," she says to herself. And sure enough, the small pile of grain which she had left on the floor inside the goose's cage grows smaller and smaller. In less than a week, amidst frequent visits from the children after school, it regains most of its strength. She then lets him out of the cage that she had temporarily placed him in, and throughout the rest of the winter the Canada goose feeds with the other fowl in the barn.

Barnyard flocks are kept on hundreds of small Chesapeake Bay farms, and during the winter thrive on a mixture of corn, oats, hay chaff and seeds picked up from the wooden barn floors. Often, however, the fowl lose weight and become somewhat pale due to the absence of sunlight, natural foods, and grit from the ground.

With the coming of the warmer weather and the spring, the barn doors are opened, and the flocks rush out with a flurry of noise and feathers onto the wet, still partially frozen ground.

And so, in the spring the Canada goose meanders out of the barn, well behind the rest of the flock. Instinctively, he spreads his wings and furiously tries to flap them again and again. But only one wing works. The other wing, the right one, barely

moves; and when he walks the wing feathers drag on the ground.
From the beginning, his strong, wild bloodlines prevail against
the bantam cocks, the mallard drakes
and the domestic grey gander.
And, by the end of the first week
out of doors when flocks
reestablish their hierarchy, the
Canada goose is the unchal-
lenged leader.

Throughout the spring
and summer and into fall, the
Canada goose, although unable
to fly, grows larger and stronger. He
begins flapping his one wing and honking early in the morning,

well before daylight, at the same time the cocks start to crow. However, he continues honking throughout the mornings and well into mid-afternoons, long after the crowing has stopped. Grandmother knows that the constant honking is the age-old call for a mate, but she also is certain that sixty miles east of the Great North South Flyway is too great a distance for the call to be heard and answered.

Chapter 5

Very early one morning in the late fall, when the frost has already begun to permeate the ground, she listens for the familiar honking intermingled with the crows of the bantams. But the honking has stopped. Her first thought is that something has happened to the Canada goose.

Perhaps a dog from a neighboring farm has jumped the fence, and when he attempted to protect the barnyard flock, he had been killed. But she knows that the aggressive game bird is more than a match for most domestic dogs, despite his crippled wing. Also, many times she has seen the three Shetland ponies which share the field with the flock chase away dogs which had ventured into the field, followed by the Canada goose running at full speed, flapping its one good wing. However, her stomach tightens when she remembers rumors that a pack of stray dogs was recently seen roaming the area.

The sun is not yet visible over the horizon when Petite Mom finally reaches the field and the makeshift shelter where the animals stay during the summer nights. To her surprise the flock is undisturbed and hardly moves as she approaches and walks through them. However, the Canada goose, which usually squats near the entrance of the shelter, is gone. She searches the entire area, into the dark shadows of the corners for nearly a half hour before she stops searching and finally realizes that the Canada goose has left.

Hesitating for a moment, Petite Mom walks over to the ponies who are already feeding. She stops beside them, strokes their scruffy winter coats and quietly talks to them. It helps to relieve the hurt that she feels at the loss of the Canada goose.

She begins to walk slowly back through the field and wonders where he has gone. When nearly to the gate, as if through instincts developed through generations of family toil on the land and with animals, she turns and walks to the far corner of the field, near the small pond where the animals and fowl water. There beside a clump of dried, uncut hay, she spies the Canada goose with its limp wing.

He is standing beside another Canada goose which is squatted in the grass, sleeping. When she approaches, he suddenly bolts from the grass toward her, with his good wing flapping. Slowly she retreats and realizes that a Canada goose hen has finally answered the ancient call.

Petite Mom reasoned that while migrating south from

over fifty miles away, the hen had heard his call, and for some unknown reason had left her own flock. Perhaps she, too, had been too weak to continue the migration and somehow had followed the same route first charted over a year before, until she had heard his honking and had landed in the field.

Later the same day both Canada geese venture to the shelter for feed. Together they spend the winter in the barn with the rest of the flock, out of the severe winter elements. In the spring after the doors are opened, they nest in the field. Both geese alternate sitting on the six eggs. And at the end of the sixth week, both leave the nest and walk to the shelter, followed by six downy offspring.

Throughout the spring and summer and into fall, the goslings feather and mature. By the time of the first frost, the six are nearly full grown and have already learned to fly. They circle the field time and time again, everyday, while the crippled gander watches from a distant corner of the field, all the while honking.

Early one morning, just before snowfly, Petite Mom and the three children who had found the bloodied and weakened goose now over two years ago, watch as the small flock of

Canada geese start their ritual. It is the first of many they will
witness during the ensuing years. Amidst the bobbing of heads
and flapping of wings, suddenly seven geese lift off
from the field and circle high above, honking. On
the second full circle, the female forms the center
of a wedge with the three goslings on each side,
and together the small flock heads south to
winter feeding grounds.

However, the crippled Canada goose
remains in the field and continues to honk
long after the flock has disappeared from
sight. When he finally stops honking, it is
late evening. Alone again, he wanders
off to the far corner of the field

where he stays for nearly a week, refusing to eat. When the other fowl from the barnyard venture near him, he aggressively chases them away with a violent display of honking and wing flapping.

Petite Mom tells the children, "He is alone and very lonely again, but perhaps in the spring, during the northern migrations, his mate may return." But because of the great distance from the flyway, the normal migration route of the Canada geese, she is not so sure.

Late at night, on the sixth day after the flock left the field and instinctively headed south to its winter feeding grounds, long after everyone is asleep, a whisper of wind carries a faint sound to the field. The Canada goose's long neck tenses. For the next five minutes he remains frozen in that position, before he begins anxiously to toss his large black head up and down. Far into the night the continuous honk of a single goose pierces the darkness.

He answers the distant honking with sounds of his own. It is less than a half hour before she lands on the ground less than two feet from her mate. She comes in very low on a straight line as if on a final approach guided by electronic radar. She is exhausted, and both birds immediately quiet down as he settles beside her.

In the morning, when Petite Mom first sees her, she is still sitting on the same spot where she landed. Her mate is grooming her as she sleeps, plucking off feathers which have loosened during her flight. By noon they are again feeding together, and that night they join the rest of the fowl and animals inside the shelter.

Each year, Petite Mom and her children, Carole, Gene, and Jon watch as nature repeats her ritual. Six goslings are born in the spring of the year in Grandmother's field. In late fall, while the crippled male waits, the hen leads her six goslings south into winter feeding grounds to join her offspring of previous years. She then returns to the same field to spend the harsh Chesapeake Bay winters with her mate. In the spring, another batch of eggs are laid and six new offspring are born. Meanwhile, whole flocks of wild Canada geese who were born here throughout the years, return to the field each spring and fall during their migrations, to eat and to rest before continuing.

Chapter 6

The sun has already turned to a bright orange and is only partially visible in the west when the three of us, Jeanne, Petite Mom and I walk slowly through the large flock of Canada Geese that blanket the entire farm. Petite Mom leads, all the while talking to the geese as she has for the past thirty years. The wild game birds hardly shuffle as they open a path through which we all walk.

"This is the same boxcar and the same shelter, and all of these Canada geese, which now number over five hundred are the same geese that were born here," I am telling my daughter.

The girl carries with her a small cup filled with grain, part of which she scatters on the ground near the flock. Suddenly, a huge black Canada goose, standing outside the others, with white feet, a very large black head and black wings, and with one wing dragging on the ground, charges the rest of the flock and chases them away before meander- ing over to the corn, and starts eating.

After awhile, Petite Mom reaches into the cup that Jeanne is holding and grabs a handful of feed. Bending over slightly, she offers the grain to 'The Master' of the flock. The large goose with the wild blood-lines lays his head in her hands and coos with a noise that sounds like the purr of a large cat.

Quietly, Petite Mom talks to him for a long time, as she has for all of those years before he slowly gobbles up the grain from the palms of her hands. Jeanne and I stare a long time at the small elderly woman with the quiet, smiling grey eyes and slightly stooped back, hand-feeding a large Canada goose with a crippled wing from two hands cupped in front of her, hands and fingers severely deformed at the joints by years of toil on the farm.

"What's his name?" Jeanne asks, alternately looking at me, Petite Mom and the goose.

"I call him 'My Crusty
with the Large Feet,' because every-
where he goes he leaves a very
large imprint of his foot; you
always know where he has
been," Petite Mom replies, as
I swing my daughter onto my
shoulders for a piggy back ride.
And together while being serenad-
ed by a large flock of wild
Canada Geese to the tune of
Chesapeake Bay Goose
Music the three of us
walk back through the
fields to the old farmhouse.

The End

Our stories are part of our folklore and we pass them on so that our children and grandchildren will better know us and also be reminded of who they are.

Acknowledgements
Neva Herrington and Ted Zieigler
Author unknown, quote on page 3

If you wish to mail a gift copy signed by the author of our Children's Series Book, "Chesapeake Bay Goose Music," please fill in information below and enclose $12.95 plus $2.00 mailing charge to
Folklore Press
Box 166
Mt. Vernon VA 22121

Name ————————————————————————————————

Address ————————————————————————————————

Sender ————————————————————————————————

Message ————————————————————————————————

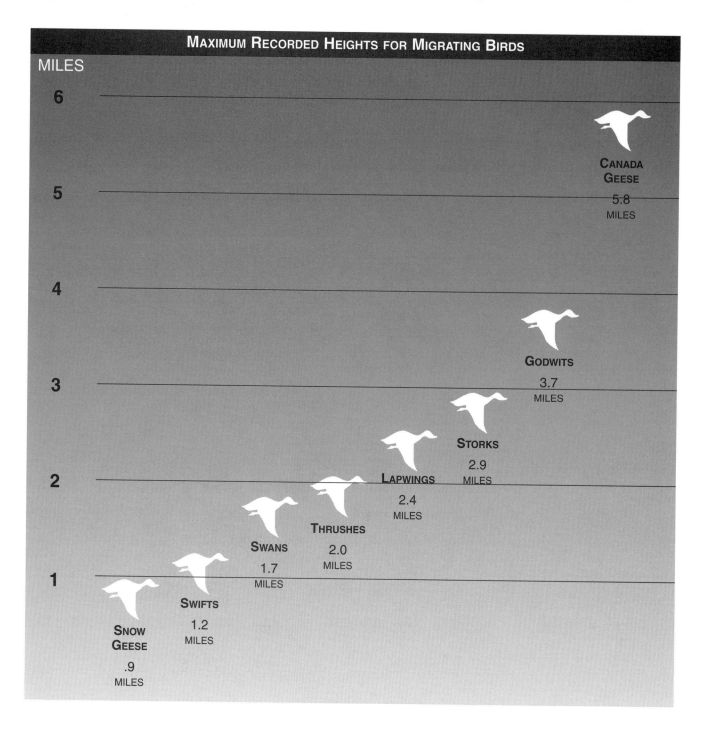

MAXIMUM RECORDED HEIGHTS FOR MIGRATING BIRDS

MILES

6

5

4

3

2

1

CANADA GEESE
5.8 MILES

GODWITS
3.7 MILES

STORKS
2.9 MILES

LAPWINGS
2.4 MILES

THRUSHES
2.0 MILES

SWANS
1.7 MILES

SWIFTS
1.2 MILES

SNOW GEESE
.9 MILES

NORTH AMERICAN FLYWAYS

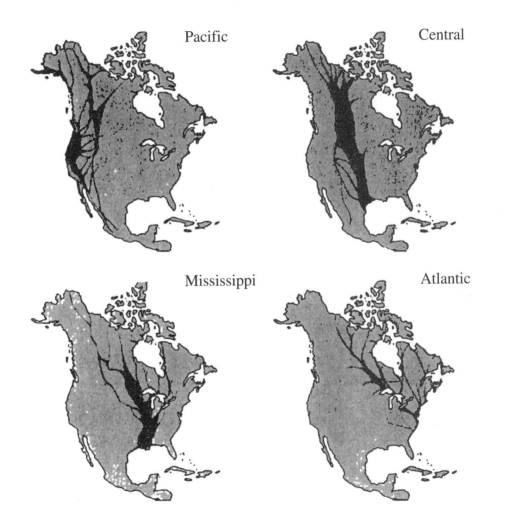

Pacific

Central

Mississippi

Atlantic